Thinking & Acting
with a Compassionate Heart

Principles & Ideas that Unlock the Human Potential

Dear Nancy!

What a blessing to meet you on this trip and this journey of life. You have a compassionate heart

with gratitude
your friend
[signature] 10/20/18

Illens Dort

Contents

Contents

♥

Acknowledgements

As an expression of gratitude to all who have come to my rescue, I devote my life in the service of my fellow human beings wherever they may be.

I am overwhelmed by profound gratitude for all who have helped me in this life:

to my dear parents - my mother, Claire Melie, who passed away 5 years ago at age 92 and my dad, Estinfort, who is approaching 99, for sacrificing all, so I could have a better future;

to my wife Fenise and all our children, for your continued support while I spent hours in the service of others;

to Giselle Valcin - my all-time favorite teacher, you taught me at a young age in Haiti what it meant to be a teacher — you always cared about the welfare of all those around you;

to George and Louise Everton, from Providence, Utah, you took my wife and me under your wing (when we first moved to the United States) and treated us as family;

to Kay and Joyce Clark, from St. George, Utah, you always made us feel welcome;

to Dave Linear, who was my first boss in the United States, you are a friend for life and your kindness and compassion provides me with an example I always try to emulate;

Acknowledgements

to Dr. David Peterson, for accepting my wife and me as your patients when we were poor students in college — you taught me that there is no stranger in the land;

to Chris Poulos and Dr. Richard Allen, for your support and encouragement in publishing this book;

to all those in this great country and Haiti, who provided tutelage and helped keep the hope alive in me;

And finally, to all who are reading this book, I express my sincere gratitude for the great influence you are having in the lives of the people around you. Your thoughts and actions matter not only to you, but also to other human beings and the planet where you live.

With much gratitude,

Illens Dort

Foreward

In a world where minds and hearts continually search for hope and enlightenment, Illens Dort offers a treasury of short aphorisms to inspire, encourage, and motivate. His core momentum of creativity is energized with this goal in mind: "What can I offer that is unique, distinctive, and inimitable for the audience to which I am reaching out?" What he produces is a wealth of brief gems that open one's vision to the higher values of life and personal connectedness with those we love. His flowing archive of sayings offers simple, yet memorable strategies to make each day more meaningful and productive. Illens is a person of great charity with a global outreach to bless many lives and families around the world. Please explore his offerings and see how your life, too, can be enriched and edified through his succinct reminders of wisdom and truth.

— R. J. Allen, Ph.D., Author and Educator

Foreward

Two of the greatest treasures in the world are human life and human potential. How many times have we seen someone from meager circumstances overcome their background and change the world for good?

Illens Dort's book is full of principles and ideas that help to unlock the human potential. It is a book that inspires, teaches, and shows the way to unlock a person's best!

Illens' personal life is an example of doing what he talks about in the book. My family and I have been fortunate to know and observe Illens and his family for many years. He has overcome difficult circumstances to raise one of the finest families we know. Not only has Illens been a success in his life, each of his children are contributing to our world in an enormously positive way.

— Steven R. Shallenberger, Author of the National Best Selling, Becoming Your Best, the 12 Principles of Highly Successful Leaders and Founder of Becoming Your Best Global Leadership

Preface

Transformational Thinking and Action

We live in a busy time. Information is coming to us like a hurricane. We are bombarded with hourly news, snapshots, Instagram pictures, Facebook comments, blog posts, and tweets. It seems like everyone is competing for our time and resources. To stop and connect with our inner-self can be a challenge. For the last four decades, I have been working on this practical process that will help you to stay focused on what matters most — I call it transformational thinking and action.

The five key principles of this process are shown in the continuous circle below.

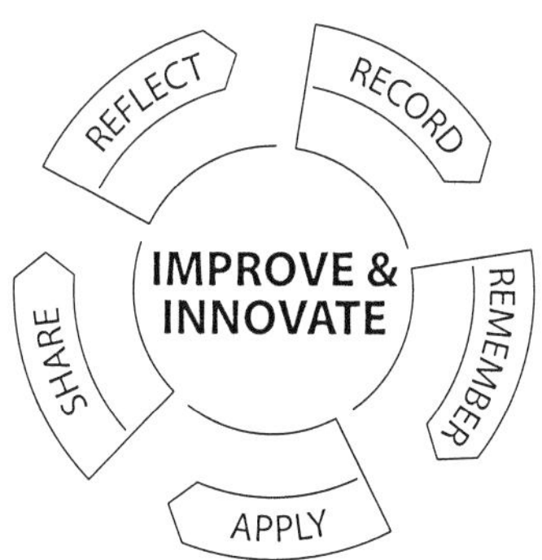

Figure 1
Transformational Thinking and Action

Reflect

Taking time to reflect daily brings us closer to our purpose in this life. We are not fugitives who are lost on the road of this mortal probation. We came to earth with a unique goal and a mission to accomplish. We were given an assignment and a road map. We accepted both the goal and the plan. At the end of each day we might find it useful to take time to ponder and reflect on the good we have done. We would benefit by pausing to contemplate the lessons we have learned and find a way to encapsulate them in a small package — a thought.

John C. Maxwell, internationally respected leadership expert, speaker, trainer, coach and New York Times Bestselling author, states, "Reflection turns experience into insight. As we pull away and we reflect our experiences can become insight if we let life-lessons be taught to us."

Some Reflective Questions

If I were called to meet my Maker today, would I be able to look Him in the eye and report that I have done my very best? Did I lift a life? Did my world or community become a better place because of me being a part of it?

Record

As we reflect on the activities of the day and discover a deeper meaning of our existence, we may want to record the feelings and thoughts that enter our hearts and minds. Recording these thoughts and feelings helps us remember them. They are given to us to help us learn and grow. Sometimes they may come to us in the middle of the night. Other times, we receive them while we're in the middle of a crisis, or during a time when we least expect them. We don't always know when they will come. What we can do is to be ready to record them. Recently, while I was at home cleaning the kitchen, I received some very clear directives on a new subject. I had to pause constantly to record them.

Recording Tools

Do you keep a pen/pencil and paper handy?

Do you have a way (cell phone, tape recorder, ipad, laptop) to record these thoughts?

Remember

Remembering is part of learning. A wise father taught his children to remember who they were and where they came from. Remembrance can help us be more grateful. It helps us know how to act when we face challenges in this life. I can't tell you how many times I have to tell myself that "To live is to love. To love is to sacrifice. Sacrifice gives more meaning to love and life." This maxim did not enter my mind and heart for nothing. It was given to me to strengthen me and help me remember my mission in life. If I did not record it and remember it, I would not have been able to apply it when I needed its comfort.

Apply

One of the favorite principles I learned from reading the Holy Scriptures is found in this statement of Peter:

"Though I speak with the tongues of men and of angels, and have not charity, I am become as sounding brass, or a tinkling cymbal. And though I have the gift of prophecy, and understand all mysteries, and all knowledge; and though I have all faith, so that I could remove mountains, and have not charity, I am nothing (1 Corinthians 13:1-2)."

Charity is a principle of action. It motivates us to do something with what we know. The same is true for positive thinking. We need to record our thoughts, so we can remember them. We remember them, so we can apply them. As we apply them, they help us be better individuals. They can remind us of our mission and responsibilities toward our fellow man.

Share

A few years ago, I was traveling with my friend, Arnauld-Joel Nakaha, on a business trip. We had a long day. We didn't believe that we had successfully accomplished our goal for that day. While we were driving and reflecting on the experiences of the day, the thought came to my mind, "We need to keep going. As difficult as the experience is, we can't cry because there is no hospital for crying babies." As we proceeded on the road, my friend asked me for my opinion about someone. The best answer that came to my mind was, "Sweet like honey and stings like a bee." My business associate laughed and got a good kick out of the two sayings.

When he was done laughing he leaned toward me and said, "Illens, where do you get them? They are so good."

I responded, "They just came to my mind."

He replied, "You need to share them."

For years, people have been encouraging to share these thoughts. I didn't want to do it. I always believed they were given to me just for my benefit and learning. Over time I realized my refusal to share them with others (not because of selfishness) may have been the reason why they stopped coming. I decided that perhaps they could benefit others. Then I decided to start sharing them in verbal conversations. The more I shared the aphorisms the more others encouraged me to publish them.

With great humility and in the hope that they may influence you for good, I offer them to you. I encourage you to take time to reflect. For, the experiences we have been given in this life prepare us to meet our Maker.

We need to record our positive thoughts and let them shape our creative actions. We need to have the discipline to remember them and apply them to bless the lives of the people around us. As you see it appropriate, may you have the courage and the humility to share them with others.

We all have within us the spring of positive thoughts and creative actions. René Descartes said, "Je pense, donc Je suis." "I think, therefore I am." From Proverbs, we learn "For as he thinketh in his heart, so is he" (Proverbs 23:7).

May we take time to cultivate our thoughts and actions daily. Let us share the fruits of that labor with others and invite them to do the same. As we partake of the fruits of goodness, we can make the world a better place for all.

Learning from the Wise

"Sow a thought and you reap an action; sow an act and you reap a habit, sow a habit and you reap a character; sow a character and you reap a destiny."

— Ralph Waldo Emerson (1803-1882)

"In my walks, every man I meet is my superior in some way, and in that I learn from him."

Ralph Waldo Emerson (1803-1882)

"Let your heart be fertile soil where great thoughts can grow and produce the fruits of strong character."

These two quotes from Emerson have a great influence on me. A thought is like a seed. Once it is planted into the soil of your heart, you have the responsibility to nourish it. When you take time to cultivate the seed, it will grow. It will transform you and the people with whom you associate. Therefore, let your heart be fertile soil where great thoughts can grow and produce the fruits of strong character.

Any time I read the second quote above, I am reminded of this old adage that I learned from my Haitian heritage. It goes like this. Two men were on a small canoe in the ocean. One man was extremely educated. He was a lawyer. The other man had no formal education.

He made his living as a fisherman, he also helped people cross the ocean to smaller islands. While the two men were together, the educated man (the passenger) asked the fisherman if he knew how to read. He responded that he did not.

The passenger replied, "Man, you don't know how to read. You are a dead man because if someone was to give you a letter that contains your death sentence you would have delivered it without knowing."

The fisherman who was a wise man and had learned many life-long lessons, paused for a moment. Then he asked the passenger, "Do you know how to swim?"

The educated man responded, "No, I don't know how to swim."

The fisherman looked at him with confidence and said, "You are the one who is a dead man. If I threw you into the ocean, you would not know how to save yourself."

I appreciate this wisdom from Ralph Waldo Emerson, "In my walks, every man I meet is my superior in some way, and in that I learn from him."

REFLECT > RECORD > REMEMBER > APPLY > SHARE

As you read each aphorism I invite you to take time to reflect on the thoughts and feelings that come to your mind and write them down. You may also want to compose your own aphorisms. Think of a friend with whom you may want to share these thoughts. You can post them on your Facebook page or tweet them. I have provided some blank pages at the back of the book for you to practice.

Some of you may have the artistic gift of illustration. If you are one of these talented people, feel free to draw the imagse that come to your mind and heart as you read these thoughts. You may want to share them with our audience. One more thing, I would appreciate it if you could share your feedback by going to my website (IllensDort. com) and comment on my weekly post. Let our community know how these maxims influence your life. Together, let us create an online Community of Transformational Thinkers and Doers. I am looking forward to hearing your thoughts and the difference you are making in your own world.

Introduction

Axioms have had a great influence on me since I was a child, growing up in Haiti. I have read some of the works of Blaise Pascal, Victor Hugo, Francois de La Rochefoucauld, Jean-Jacques Rousseau and many other great philosophers. Over the years, I have also become acquainted with profound quotes from people that you and I associate with on a daily basis. We don't usually quote these people because they are not famous. Their ideas and mentorship often stay with us for many years.

When I face a unique situation and I try to find a way to express my feelings, it seems more comfortable to put them in a simple package — a maxim. Sometimes these aphorisms come to me while I am conversing with someone. Other times they enter my heart after hours of deep reflection.

After sharing these adages with friends and relatives, many of them encouraged me to publish them. Some have gone so far as to ask me to share the circumstances that led to these thoughts. I encourage you to read each aphorism and pause to contemplate how it might inspire your life before moving on to the description that shows how it has inspired mine.

I encourage you to share your thoughts and experiences, so others can learn from them. Let the people in your circle of influence know how these aphorisms have influenced your life and actions for good. May you continue to press forward and spread rays of sunshine until your mission in this life is completed.

Visit my site: www.IllensDort.com, to share your comments and feedback.

Thinking & Acting with a Compassionate Heart

SUNSHINE

> Let the sunshine in your soul keep your body warm while walking in the rain.

As we travel through the journey of life, we often go through hills and valleys. We enjoy sunny days and also experience some cloudy and rainy seasons. We celebrate the birth of precious souls who come to our families. We also mourn at the departure of our loved ones. Some may experience these contrasting feelings during the same season.

Life offers us some opportunities for success. Life also serves as a laboratory for learning, improvement, and growth. On some occasions, we may find ourselves at the bottom of the mountain or trailing behind a long line of fellow travelers and wonder if we will ever catch up to them. Other times we may wonder if it is even worth it to keep trying.

During our journey, here in mortality, we may experience days when we feel that this hurricane that seems to always hit our homes will never stop. It is during these moments that we need to focus on just the next step, while reaching deep into our souls to find the courage to continue to move forward. In these moments of difficulties, it is wise to remember that the sunshine that we cultivate in our hearts will always be there to keep us warm and provide the nutrients that our souls need to continue strong on this journey of this mortal life.

Therefore, "Let the sunshine in your soul keep your body warm while walking in the rain." As you do so, you may also find that you have a little extra sunshine that you can freely share with a friend, a member of your family, or someone you meet on your path.

Your Thoughts

FAITH

> Problems that can be solved offer us an opportunity to exercise our mental capacity.
>
> Problems that can't be solved offer us an opportunity to exercise our faith.

How we approach the challenges we face in this life can determine in great measure how we appreciate our journey in mortality.

I remember how much in my youth I enjoyed solving math and physics problems. It was a fun activity for me. I would spend many hours working on these problems. There were times I worked on them late in the nights until my brain could no longer focus. I knew if I worked hard enough and applied all the fundamentals, I would eventually solve even the most difficult problem.

I studied the formulas and practiced them over and over. I even created my own formulas and patterns for problem solving. They helped me be prepared to tackle complex problems. I discovered that a great part of being able to solve problems was the ability to:

1) understand the root cause of the problem

2) know and identify which formulas or tools can help

3) tackle the problem one piece at a time

I can still remember how happy I was when I finally arrived at the solution. It was a great feeling of accomplishment and excitement.

Once we find the solution to a problem, we no longer worry about that problem. Therefore, a problem that can be solved is not a problem. It becomes an exercise. It simply offers us an opportunity to exercise our mental capacity.

We sometimes face problems in life with no known solutions. How do we approach these problems? Knowing that God is all knowing and is the creator and author of this universe can give us the confidence to go to Him for solutions. It is refreshing to know that every problem in this life has a solution. We need to know the source of the problem and the root cause. We also need to understand what known formulas we have at our disposal. Before or after we have done all that we can, we can confidently and patiently call on our Heavenly Father for help. He is the Master of all masters. He also desires to help us. But we need to do our part and study the problem. And finally, ask in faith for his help and be willing to accept His solution.

Everyday try to do your very best. And to the Lord, leave the rest.

Your Thoughts

____

____

____

LOVE

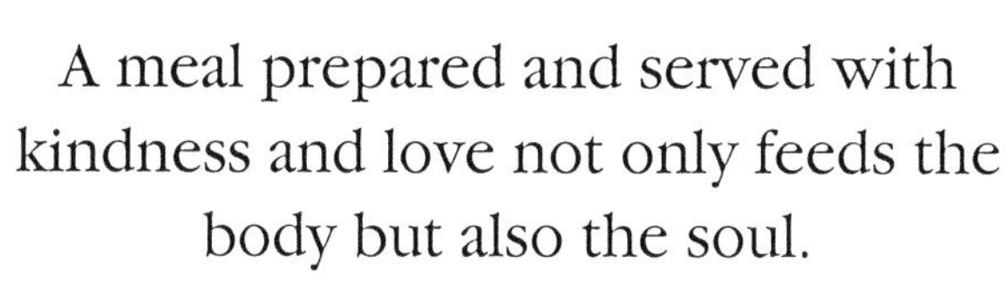

I love to cook. There were times my children told me that I was being a little too creative with my cooking skills. We love when the family gathers together for dinner. Now that five of them are married, we also enjoy the company of their spouses and our grandchildren.

One day after I spent a couple of good hours preparing a meal, I was a bit tired and anxious to start eating. The children were having a great time visiting with one another. After a couple of invitations to come to the table for dinner, I showed a sign of impatience. I was thinking in my mind, "I spent a great deal of time preparing the food. I don't like cold food. On top of that, I am ready to eat (meaning I am really hungry) — let's get going." One of our daughters kindly asked me a simple question, "Dad, did you eat something?" That question caused me to ponder and reflect on my behavior for I knew what she meant.

It was during that moment I realized that I forgot two key ingredients; love and kindness. The meal was delicious and the table was well garnished. But, I could have extended the invitation with a little more love, kindness, and patience. Since that day, I learned my lesson. When I cook, I make sure I eat something, so I can control my emotions. I don't let my stomach control my spirit and my heart. I also make sure that I don't leave out these two ingredients; love and kindness.

LOVE

Love is the universal language that we all speak and understand perfectly.

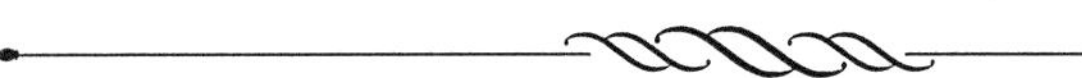

Love can't be purchased. It can only be given and received freely and voluntarily.

We serve those we love. We come to love those we serve.

Human beings are born with love and to love. Some of us are taught and trained to hate others.

Your Thoughts

____

____

LONELINESS AND LOVE

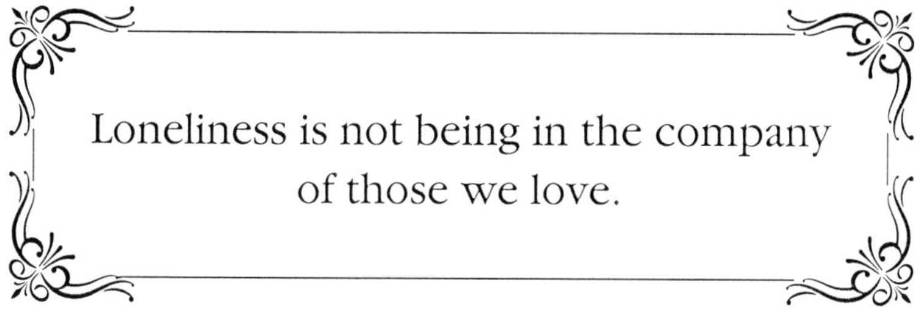

Loneliness is a state of mind and a disposition of the heart. There are always people around us. They may not be in the same room as we are. We just need to keep them safe in the chamber of our hearts. We are always in the company of someone, some animals, some plants, some flowers, the earth, the birds, the mountains, the ocean etc.

A wonderful lady, who lived to see the age of 96, shared with my wife and me how she talked to her flowers. Her husband had left this mortal probation over 30 years before she passed away.

Another friend who had spent 2 years in Haiti for his church commented on how frequently he would speak to his animals, so he would not forget the language he had learned there. At that time, he was living on a farm in a remote location of Utah. He loved the language and the Haitian people so much that he didn't want to forget the language. He said, "I knew the animals couldn't speak back, but they were great companions to practice my Creole with.

When we feel lonely, most of the time it's not because we don't have other human beings around us. It's more often because we are thinking about not being with someone we really care about or who loves us. If you ever find yourself in that state, here are a few suggestions for you to consider:

- **Know** you are never alone. You have a Father in Heaven who watches over you constantly. He is the closest person to you. You can talk to him any time and in any place. He speaks your language perfectly.

- **Look** for others that may be having the same feeling. If you reach out to them, then you can help each other.

- **Enjoy** the beauty of the creation. The mountains, the birds, the animals, the flowers, the plants, and the ocean are constant and dependable companions one can have. They too, can comfort you in your moment of solitude.

- **Meditate** and reflect. You can use that moment to meditate, to reflect and to connect with your inner-self. It can be a valuable time to feel the protecting spirit of unseen angels who are around you.

- **Remember.** The number of people who are in your company may be greater than the ones who are not with you. Do you have the eyes to see that unseen legion and the heart to feel their presence?

- **Read.** A great book can be an awesome companion. I remember as a young man in high school, there were few months when I couldn't go to school because my parents did not have the funds to pay for school. I stayed home. I started to feel lonely. I missed going to school. I borrowed uplifting books from a neighbor who had access to a French Library in

Haiti. These books served as solid companions and trusted advisors. I felt I could connect with the authors. They were my friends even though many of them had already died or lived in a different continent.

- **Serve.** What more can I say about service. There are always plenty of opportunities for service. You don't even need to leave your community. Serve where you are. "Service is the safe treasury that always pays dividends on any investment deposited."

- **Write** in your journal or just write. Use that time to be creative and productive. Let your mind, heart, and will come together. Something amazing can happen when you are able to combine these three together. You can innovate, create, and transform.

Add your own ideas

____

____

____

____

____

____

____

LONELINESS AND LOVE

He who truly loves his fellowmen will never be lonely. For he will always have a companion in his heart.

Add your own ideas

____

____

____

____

SACRIFICE AND LOVE

> To live is to love. To love is to sacrifice. Sacrifice gives more meaning to love and life.

During the last few years, I made some major sacrifices as I was working on a humanitarian project with Lift a Life as the CEO of the organization. Humanitarian work requires time, dedication, commitment, and sacrifices. The results are not always apparent and immediate. The organization was running at that time solely on volunteer help. Everyone was making incredible sacrifices. We all knew we were building something that would last a long time and the benefits were entirely for the less-fortunate people that we cared about.

During these years, it became clear to me that many people who had great influence on others understood the meaning of life, love, and sacrifice. These three active words play an integral part in their lives. They lived a life of love for their fellowmen and made huge sacrifices to demonstrate that love.

It doesn't matter where you live, you will find these people in your society. Some are very famous. Many others live a simple life and are only known to the people whose lives they have touched. As you are reading this thought you may be thinking of someone who exemplifies the meaning of these three powerful words. You may be one of them.

Sacrifice requires time, talent and energy. In many instances we may be asked to put all we have on the alter. Good Samaritans always do good deeds with the gifts that they possess.

Your Thoughts

____

____

____

____

____

____

____

SACRIFICE AND LOVE

Treat everything, even the earth, with respect. For it was made out of love and sacrifice.

Your Thoughts

____

____

____

♥

NO STRANGER IN THE LAND

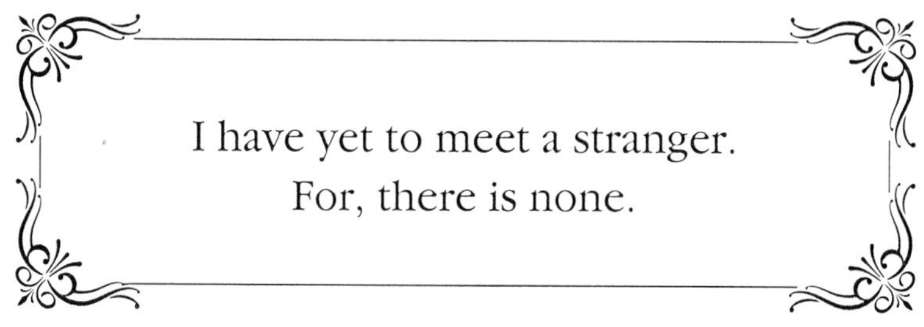

In the Merriam-Webster Dictionary, stranger is defined as "a person or thing that is unknown or with whom one is unacquainted." The reverse of this definition is also true. Once we take time to know someone or to be acquainted with that person, that person is no longer a stranger. The question remains, how long does it take us to know someone?

Some years ago, I was attending a networking event. There were eight of us at the table. We had not met before. We were given two minutes each to share something about ourselves and briefly talk about our businesses. Before we were done, I no longer felt I was in the company of strangers. Within a few minutes of interaction with one another, I had a different feeling about these people. What I thought of them was only a precipitated judgement. Once I devoted the time to get to know them I was no longer a stranger to them; and them to me. They were friends that I had to cultivate. Changing the way I think of others helps me be more mindful of how I need to treat them.

PERFECTION

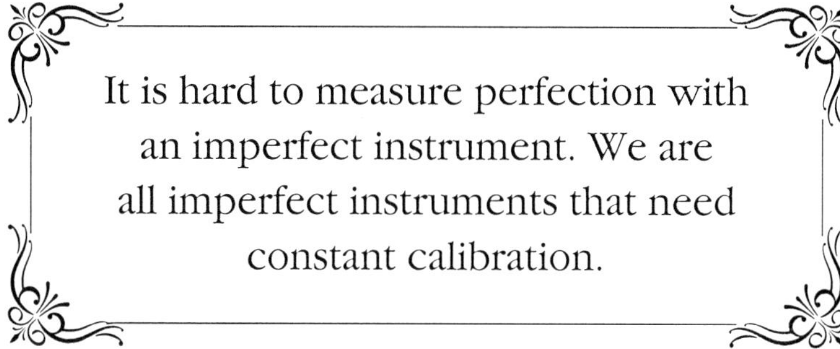

As a student in the electronic engineering program I learned a very important principle about having the right instrument to measure current, voltage and power etc. Not only was it important to have the right instrument, it was also imperative to make sure that the instrument was properly calibrated. If the instrument was off, the reading was also off. This is also true for a scale. If the scale is off and the needle is not centered to zero, the reading of the weight can't be accurate.

As human, we may have a tendency to quickly judge others when we ourselves walk imperfectly. When we try to do a little better in our own lives we can become more patient with others.

Your Thoughts

____

____

____

____

____

PERFECTION

Don't worry if you are not perfect. For none of us are. But we all can try to be a little bit better each day.

This world is a perfect place for imperfect people to dwell.

Your Thoughts

____

____

____

____

____

____

____

____

____

SERVICE

> Service is the safe treasury that always pays dividend on any investment deposited.

Paying forward is a forward thinking and action principle that people who cultivate a compassionate heart live by. When our heart is filled with gratitude, we look forward to adding value to those around us. We don't worry; we simply ask what we can do to serve others.

As a young student in elementary school in Haiti, I struggled with math. I had to work hard every day to get a decent grade in math. This problem went on for five years. I didn't know what to do. I thought math was just a hard subject. If I couldn't do well it must have been the way it was. I lived with the weakness for many years.

Just before I began the last year of elementary school I felt a need to seek help. I wanted to make sure I did everything I could to be ready for the regional test. It was a test all students had to take before they could go to high school. I didn't worry about my ability to pass these tests. My goal was to be among the top 10 percent, or even better, the number one student among thousands of participants. Scoring high in math was crucial if I were to achieve this lofty goal.

Miss Giselle Valcin was the teacher of that class. She was known for her ability to get students ready for the final exam. She knew well all the subjects she taught. Miss Valcin had never been married and had no children. She was a single lady who made teaching her career and calling in life. She was a passionate and devoted teacher. All the students and their parents loved and respected her. She also had a reputation of being fair and firm.

I knew at that time if there was someone who could help me overcome my weakness in math, Ms. Valcin would be that person. All I had to do was to ask. I spent the entire summer working on math and physic problems, but that wasn't enough. While I could solve many math problems, I knew something was missing.

So, during the first day of class I went to Miss Valcin and told her about my goal and my weakness in math. She could not believe that I struggled in math because I was always among the top students in my class. That reputation of being diligent and intelligent preceded me. However, I told her that I had to work hard to earn a decent grade in math. I also told her that I was ready to do whatever is necessary to overcome this weakness.

She reassured me that it was not too late. She talked to me about a plan that would help me. The plan required that I come to school early (one hour before school) and stay late (one hour after school). These times were reserved for students who needed help on any subject they struggled with. I agreed and I was so excited. After six weeks receiving one-on-one attention I overcame the problem.

My fear of math was gone and my confidence increased. The year went very well. I took the test and did extremely well. Even though I was not the number one student, I finished among the top 10 percent. More importantly, I became a big fan of math.

As a way to show gratitude for the help I had received from her, and to help other students who didn't like math, I offered to tutor these students for free. I did that through all my high school years.

During those years I tutored many young people. Some of them were my age, while others were younger and a few who were older. While I was living in Port-au-Prince, I had the privilege of tutoring a young girl who struggled with math, and specifically geometry and trigonometry.

She was not alone. Geometry and trigonometry were not friendly to many students in high schools. But, with what I have learned from Ms. Giselle Valcin, I knew exactly what to do. I offered to help her and developed a plan. I tutored her for two consecutive years for free. She was in one grade below me.

I was in my first year at the Science Faculty in Port-au-Prince. One of the top two faculties in Haiti, with the medical school being the number one in terms of toughness and difficulty to be admitted.

One of my goals was to teach math in high school. As a university student, one could teach one or two classes in high school if the student knew the subject very well. I decided to apply for a part-time teaching job. Some schools had tests you were required to take before they would consider you. I did well in all the tests, but I had one problem — I was young.

The principals were confident that I could teach the subject, but they weren't sure that I could handle the high school students. Many of the students were closer to my age. That wasn't a problem for me, but I couldn't convince the principals to give me a shot. I was somewhat disappointed. I knew I was capable of teaching the subject and I also knew that I could handle the students. I loved to teach. I also loved to help others, especially students who could not attend high-paying private schools.

One evening I was talking to my friend Getude. She asked me what my plan was for the new school year. She knew I was good at math and passionate about teaching, so she suggested that I consider looking for a part-time job utilizing my skills. Making a few bucks to help me buy books and cover the cost of transportation to go to school was also appealing to me.

I told her that I tried and wasn't successful.

She asked me where I applied.

I shared with her a few schools, one of which was College Isidor Jean-Louis.

In Haiti, we refer to high schools as colleges. To my pleasant surprise, she told me she knew the principal. Mr. Isidor Jean-Louis, the owner and principal of the school, was a good friend of her parents. Her parents knew me very well. Her parents and my friend called Mr. Jean-Louis and gave me the highest recommendation. They talked about my character and how disciplined I was. They told him he was missing out on a great teacher. They convinced him that he didn't have to worry about my ability to handle these students.

The next day following their conversation, I received a call from Mr. Isidor who invited me to revisit with him. He told me how impressed he was with the recommendation that he had received from my friend and her parents. He offered me the job on the spot. I was so happy. I needed the job. I also wanted to help these students and make a difference in their lives. Having a teacher who respected them and who could relate to their struggles could make a huge difference.

I worked hard every day to make sure I was at the top of my game. I treated each student with respect. They knew I cared about them.

They also knew that my desire was to help them. They in turn showed me the same respect. I never had to worry about handling the class. They behaved respectfully during my class.

Another lesson that I learned was that service will always pay dividends. I tutored many students for many years and never received any payments. I never expected anything from any of them. I did the kind deed as a way to help others in need and to express gratitude to those who had helped me.

Your Thoughts

____

____

____

____

____

____

____

____

____

____

____

____

____

SERVICE

> Today is your day to live and serve others. For tomorrow may never come in this life.

In June of 2015, I was in the Dominican Republic with International Aid Serving Kids, a nonprofit organization that focuses on health care and vocational training for people who live in abject poverty in Haiti and the Dominican Republic. We had a wonderful week serving together.

On the last day of service, Friday, June 12, I received a text from my wife informing me that our oldest son, Bedford, was in the hospital in intensive care. She explained that he had collapsed while he was in the gym and had to be brought back to life. Luckily for him, he had a friend who was there who started CPR. There was also a doctor in the gym that worked on him. They called the paramedic team.

They had to use an extensive resuscitation technique to revive him several times while in the ambulance. When he got to the hospital and regained consciousness he was wondering where he was and how he got there. He didn't recall any of the activity that took place. His ribs were extremely sore due to the extreme pressure they had to apply to get his heart to start beating again.

He is now doing extremely well. He often joked about the fact that he had a new birth. He celebrates two birthdays — the day he was born and the day he was revived.

You may know someone who is dear to you who has left this mortal probation in a "clin d'oeil" (twinkling of an eye). When that happens we often wish we had taken time to let them know how much we loved them.

Your Thoughts

____

____

____

____

SERVICE

Serve the low and serve the high because we are all in the middle.

If you are not helping others you are not growing. If you stop growing, you will be diminished.

Your Thoughts

____

____

____

____

SERVICE

If you learn how to create things and serve others you will never be poor.

❤

Your Thoughts

____

____

____

____

____

____

____

❤

LIFT A LIFE

> You can't put another person down
> without lowering yourself as well.

We are in this world together for a reason. Without the support of one another we would not have been able to survive.

Your Thoughts

____

____

____

____

____

____

____

LIFE

Don't be so preoccupied about making
a living that you forget to live.

This life is like driving on an interstate road.
We must keep our eyes open and remain alert
at all times with both hands on the steering
wheel — and not leave our bright lights on
until we reach our final destination.

Lift a Life. Inspire a Community.
Elevate our World

Your Thoughts

____

____

____

____

LIFE

Birth, life, and death are precious gifts that we all need to treasure. They are elements of a perfect plan.

Learn to live a good life.
For, there is no end to life.

Day and night are a type of life and death.
They transition from one to another.

Your Thoughts

____

____

____

____

____

____

LIFE

Take great care of your body daily. It does the
same thing for you every second
of your mortal life.

If you are taking your life in the wrong
direction, you can make a "volte face."

Fearing death does not stop it from happening.
It only makes this life less enjoyable.

Your Thoughts

____

____

____

____

____

____

____

LIFE

The fact is we all will die one day. Preparing for that day by serving others helps us live life to its fullest.

If we want to remember and feel how precious life is, all we have to do is to hold an infant in our arms.

Practice is as real as any real thing you have done in this life. Do your very best when you practice something.

Your Thoughts

____

____

____

____

____

____

LIFE

This life is like flying in an airplane. There are several seats. Each seat is given a name and a value: first class seats, cockpit seats, coach seats etc. But, the beauty of it is that all travelers enter and exit the plane through the same gate.

If you feel you have reached the pinnacle of your life, enjoy it while you are there, because this is not your permanent residence.

We live a life of abundance.
It starts with the generosity of the heart.

Your Thoughts

____

____

____

____

KINDNESS

Always try to be kind and considerate to others. For you never know which soul might need your compassionate heart.

Try not to offend any human being. Be kind to all. For you never know which soul may need your comforting words.

When you think about throwing the kitchen sink at someone, think first about how you would feel if someone were to push you into a septic tank.

Your Thoughts

KINDNESS

A man can rob you of everything you have.
But, he can't take away the kindness you share
with others and the knowledge that you store
in your brain.

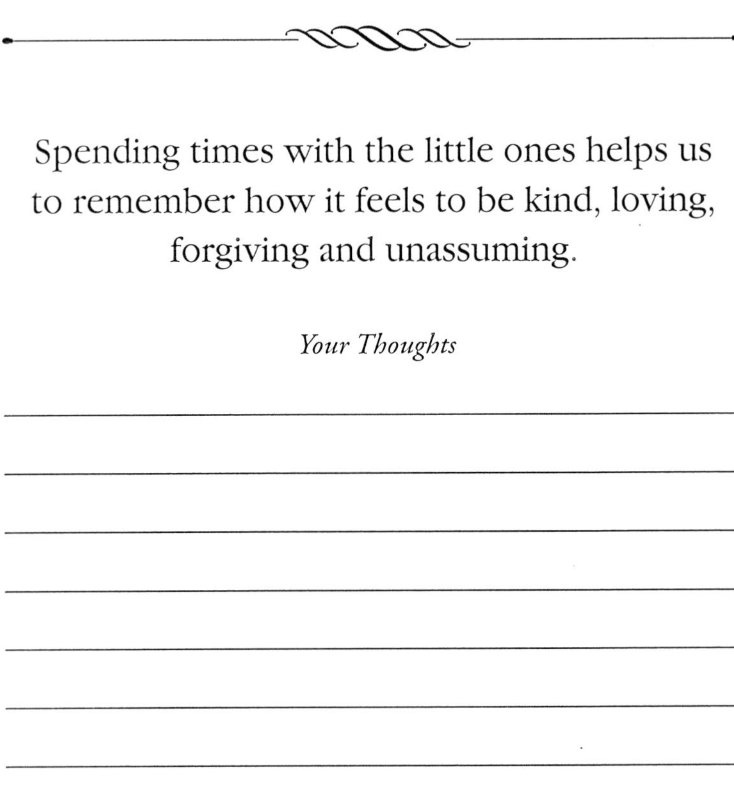

Spending times with the little ones helps us
to remember how it feels to be kind, loving,
forgiving and unassuming.

Your Thoughts

____

____

____

____

____

____

____

GENUINE SMILE

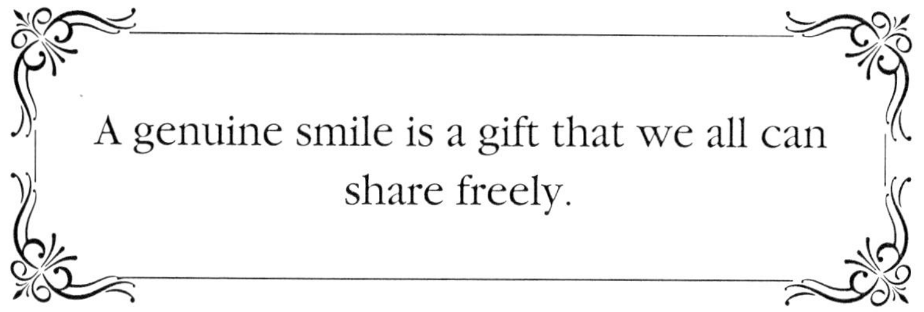

A genuine smile is a gift that we all can share freely.

One beautiful morning, I was on my way to work. I was driving on 800 North in Orem, Utah. There was a car coming from the opposite direction. In the back seat was sitting a child looking out the window. She kindly waved at me and smiled. The smile was priceless. It was genuine and authentic. I continued to drive. But, I will never forget this kind act. She made my day. I was probably thinking about a long day at work.

While I don't clearly remember the mood I was in before that moment, I can remember how I felt after she shared her smile. I totally embraced the rest of the day with a much more positive attitude. A child had brightened my day by simply sharing her smile with me. Since that day, I make it a practice to share a smile with others as I come in contact with them.

Your Thoughts

____

____

____

PASSION AND COMPASSION

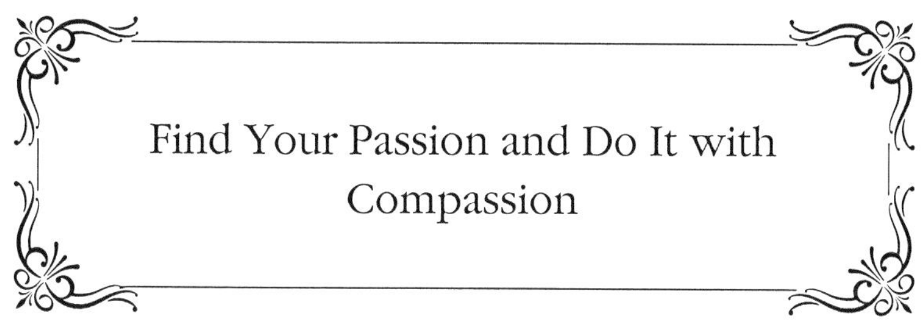

Find Your Passion and Do It with Compassion

Each human being is born with some innate gifts, talents, and capacities. These skills allow us to progress in this life and to make contributions to the community where we live. Peter Drucker who is known as the father of modern management shared the four C's that all leaders must possess. They include competence, character, compassion and community.

While the first two (competence and character) seem to require more self-disciplined and personal improvement, they can also be influenced by the other two — compassion and community. These four elements of excellent leadership support one another.

As we take time to identify our strengths and passions; we need to work hard to be the best we can be; we also increase our capacity to make meaningful contributions to our community. Imagine that you are living on an island all by yourself. You possess all the gifts and talents that a person can be endowed with.

You diligently cultivate these gifts. You made the all-star team – one man team. The whole island reveres and respects you. You are the king of the entire island. But, you have no subordinates. You have dominion over all the animals, the fowls of the air, and the fishes in the oceans. The lilies of the fields even bow at your presence. How wonderful that type of life would be? The answer is, not so wonderful.

For example, what if you were the greatest composer in the world and had no one to enjoy and appreciate your compositions? What if you were the greatest basketball player on the planet and there was no team to play for? What if you were playing on a team and the arena was completely empty? We need our community. Our community needs us. Albert Pike says it best: "What we do for ourselves dies with us. What we do for others and the world remains and is immortal."

It goes without saying that no one who is reading this article lives on an island alone. We all belong to a community. That community may be comprised of the members of our families, our work group, our team or department, our town or city, our country, and our world.

Our community also includes our customers and other people we associate with. In our quest to develop our gifts and become more competent we must also remember that we need the support of our community. We too need to show more gratitude and respect to the members of our community and for the environment itself.

Passion is about oneself. Compassion is about others. This definition offers a simple illustration of how they differ one from another. The similarity is that passion is embedded in compassion. To put it in a simple form, one cannot have compassion without having any passion. Our gifts, talents, and capacities are tools that help us better serve our communities. Our desire to serve our community can influence our desire to increase our competence in a specific field. That is a thought worth pondering.

Let us always strive to find our passion and perform our acts with more compassion. For "We are in this world together for a reason. Without the support of one another we would not have been able to survive."

Your Thoughts

____

____

____

____

____

____

____

____

____

____

____

PASSION AND COMPASSION

> A meal shared with someone in need is the most satisfying meal one can eat.

My father and my mother have been great examples of serving and caring for people in need. They lived in a culture that embraced the community. The village was small enough that everyone knew everyone. Sharing their resources, specially meals, were part of their daily lives. They extended their help even to people they had met for the first time. I watched my parents repeatedly offer part of their subsistance to strangers. As a child, most of the time I thought that was cool. There were other times I wondered if there would be enough for us children.

One day, while working on the farm far away from our home, we began cooking our lunch. When the food was ready, my father served it to his workers and us. Then he directed my attention to another man who was working by himself in his own small piece of land a few blocks away from us.

Father told me, "Son, I have not seen any sign of fire over there (because we used wood to make fire to cook), this man probably does not have any food. Please take this plate to him." I obediently performed the assignment. I will never forget how grateful that person was when I brought the meal to him. He thanked me and asked me to thank my dad for his kindness and for sharing the meal.

Then my dad kindly taught me an important lesson that day; first by example and second with these few words; "If you are blessed with enough food for yourself and your family, you are also blessed with enough to share." He paused and added these words of wisdom, "A meal shared with someone in need is the most satisfying meal one can eat." He was right then and he is still right today.

I have observed both my father and my mother applying this principle. As a testament of their kindness and thoughtful kind acts, when my mother passed away nearly five years ago, a priest traveled from afar to attend her funeral. When my sister introduced me to the priest, I probed to understand better why he traveled so far to pay tribute to my mother.

My sister told me that he wanted to express his gratitude. When he was a child he did not have a place to live and had no food. Mother invited him into her home and took care of him until he could find a job and take care of himself. Mother supported him for many years. And yet, in those days my parents did not have a big home. They were getting by with limited resources.

Your Thoughts

____

____

____

____

____

____

PASSION AND COMPASSION

Compassion is the good deed we do
to alleviate the suffering of others.

We are in this world together for a reason.
Without the support of one another we
wouldn't have been able to survive.

To show compassion is an expression
of gratitude.

Your Thoughts

____

____

____

____

____

____

____

PASSION AND COMPASSION

To be compassionate is to be kind and considerate to others. It is to lift, to sustain, to support, to enrich, to inspire, and to elevate the people around us.

Time is a gift. Share it.

Your Thoughts

LEADERSHIP

> Leadership is not an activity that takes place in the future. Leadership is an everyday behavior and action.

Leadership is about taking people from where they are to where they need to be, even when they may not believe that they can get there.

Leadership is about transforming our lives and the lives of those around us.

Your Thoughts

____

____

____

____

____

LEADERSHIP

A leader is someone who transforms his own
life so he can help others do the same.

Builders and innovators don't build things only
with what they have and what they can see;
but with also what they can imagine and with
their ability to inspire others to participate in
the building process.

Your Thoughts

____

____

____

____

____

____

____

HUMILITY

Humility is an inner strength that we all
have. But, only few of us have taken the
time to discover and cultivate
that strength.

Be humble and gracious in your moments
of victory and success, so you won't be too
discouraged in your days of defeat and failure.
For we all will have these moments in this life.

Don't pray to God to bless you with the
material things you need to help others. Pray
that He will bless the poor and the needy in
any way He can. If you desire to help Him, be
ready and be humble that you can.

Your Thoughts

FORGIVENESS

> Forgive others, not because they always deserve it, but because they and you need the cleansing power of forgiveness.

When I was twelve or thirteen years old I had a little disagreement with a lady in our community. I thought I was treated unkindly and I retaliated. The incident was reported to my father who disciplined me. At that time, I didn't think nor believe I did anything wrong. But, my behavior (not being kind) was not in harmony with the principles that my parents taught me. As a payback for getting me in trouble with my parents I decided that I would never say hi to her. The best way to do that was to avoid her all together. If I saw her coming, I would turn my back and go the opposite direction or take a different route.

I was comfortable with behaving this way for about 8 years. Eventually, a silent mutual agreement was formed to never speak to each other again. I thought she did not like me and will probably never like me. For a long time our arrangement did not bother me. After all, I had a lot of people who liked me.

In the early part of 1983, a little over 8 years since that incident had happened, I had a change of heart that constituted a greater change of behavior (even though I was always a good person). I decided to have peace and a place in my heart for all.

One Sunday, after not having seen this lady for over 3 years, I found myself crossing her path. Without thinking about it I walked by her without saying hi. This time I reacted out of habit; I just responded as I had for so long.

Suddenly, I felt a sense of urgency to return and approach her. While it was uncomfortable at first, I took courage and I followed the prompting of a greater spirit of kindness. I rushed to her and looked her in the eyes and offered my sincere apology. I told her that for many years I wanted to apologize to her. But, I did not have the courage.

In addition, I was not sure she would accept my apology. I asked her to forgive me for my behavior. At that point, I had already forgiven her in my heart. I just needed an occasion to show it by my action. She responded with the sweetest words that a forgiving soul can utter. She said, "my son, I too have been waiting for you to talk to me. I wished I had the courage to reach out to you."

Oh, how great it felt. I conquered the enemy of my soul. She was not my enemy. I was not her enemy. The enemy was my attitude toward her and the feelings I harbored in my heart for so many years. We both were friends who needed to be liberated by the power of forgiveness.

I walked back home that afternoon with such a great joy and peace. My burden had been lifted. I had found my friend.

Since that moment, our mortal paths have not crossed again. She was the age of my mother. She probably already left this world. I am so glad I had the courage to make that move; first to forgive her and second to ask her to forgive me.

FORGIVENESS

An unforgiving heart is one that lacks oxygen.

Breathe the air of forgiveness. Let it penetrate your lungs and your heart and fill your whole body with life and energy.

Don't try to get even; for it is a very high bar that you don't want to reach. But, try to be forgiving — for this is a much more achievable and worthy goal.

Your Thoughts

____

____

____

____

____

GRATITUDE

A grateful heart is a healthy heart.
Let your gracious heart illuminate and
bless the ground where you stand.

Be grateful that you have a job to do.
For no one owes it to you.

Be grateful that you have people who work
for you and with you. If you could do it all
by yourself you probably would not have
needed them.

Your Thoughts

GRATITUDE

If you feel you have hit rock bottom,
be grateful that you have reached that point,
because it can only get better from here.

Your Thoughts

____

____

____

____

♥

HAPPINESS

If you are not happy with what you have,
you will never be happy with what
you don't have.

Your Thoughts

____

____

____

____

♥

PERSEVERANCE

When you face a tough situation, and feel like you want to give up and cry your heart out; remember that you are not alone and there is no hospital for crying babies. Take courage and keep on trying.

Your Thoughts

____

____

____

____

♥

LIMITATIONS

Let us not be consumed by our limitations. We all have them. We need to work with them and work around them. They are given to us for our benefits and to keep us humble.

Your Thoughts

____

____

____

____

LIMITATIONS

Don't let the things you can't do keep you from accomplishing the things you can do.

Your Thoughts

____

____

____

____

____

____

CONFIDENCE

> Confidence comes from knowing that, it
> doesn't matter what happens to us,
> God has a perfect plan for each one of us.

Ten Things That Help Me Be More Confident

Two months ago, a young friend of mine asked me to share thoughts that help me be more confident. His request provided me with an opportunity to self-reflect. Here are the eight beliefs I shared with him. After deep moments of reflection, I added two more.

First: I Believe in God - I know that I am a child of God. He cares about me. He knows me. He is my father. I was born with goodness and intelligence.

Second: I am a Child of God - I know who I am. I know where I come from. I embrace that fact. I have a brother, in Jesus Christ, who will never forsake me.

Third: Worth of Souls - Because of the first two reasons I understand that all human beings have worth – the worth of soul is important in the sight of God. I respect all human beings.

Fourth: Purpose - I know I am here on earth to make a contribution to society. I know why I am here on this earth. I feel a sense of purpose in me being here on earth.

Fifth: Hard Work - Since I know that my life has a purpose I work hard to educate myself, so I can accomplish this mission. I practice a never-give-up mindset.

Sixth: Humility - I remain humble in my days of success and plenty, so I don't get too discouraged in my days of defeats and my days of needs.

Seventh: Attitude of Gratitude - When things get tough, I look toward God and see all the good he has done for me. I try to be grateful even in the midst of trials.

Eighth: Outward Mindset - I look at life with an outward mindset. Life is not all about me. I surround myself with people who have the same mindset. I try to lift a soul who needs my help. I allow others to lift my soul as well.

Ninth: Positive Self-talk - Every morning I wake up and tell myself, "Life is good." I remind myself that I am a child of God. I speak kind words to others and I take time to enjoy the small victories of the day.

Tenth: Perseverance - We are here to finish the race. Sometimes we will fall, fumble, and make some faux pas, but we need to get back on our feet and keep on going.

I understand the greater plan. I know where I came from. I know why I am here. I know where I am going. This knowledge of the greater plan helps me in both my spiritual and temporal time of needs.

Confidence comes from knowing that, it doesn't matter what happens to us, God has a perfect plan for each one of us. The plan helps me better understand where we came from, why we are here, and where we are going. God is the architect of this plan. Jesus is the perfect example of this plan. We can have complete trust in both of them.

♥

Your Thoughts

____

____

____

____

____

____

♥

BUSINESS

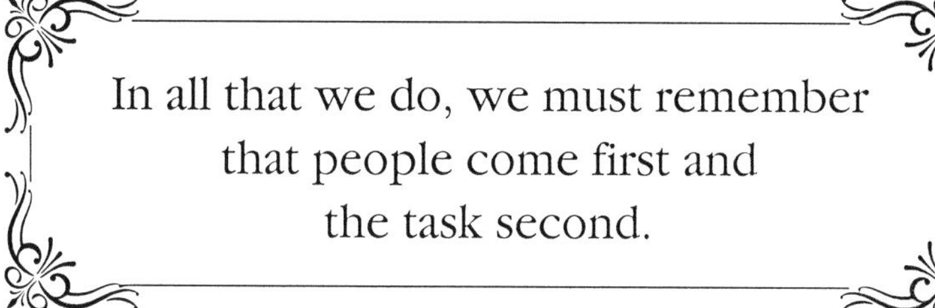

In the late spring of 1997, after being in this great country for over 10 years, we decided to take a trip to Haiti as a family. My wife and I have six young children. The youngest was only 5 months old and we had our hands full. We were excited about the opportunity to introduce our young family to our parents and siblings. We had been waiting for that trip for so long. The four children who could understand the meaning of that trip were also excited.

At that time, I was working for Novell. The office was within a walking distance from my home in Orem, Utah. I had a wonderful manager by the name of Todd Abney — a compassionate leader. A leader who understood that people matter. I had the privilege of working for Todd in two different capacities. During that moment, Todd was the manager of the technical team. He had several technical support engineers who reported to him.

I talked to Todd about taking days off, so I could visit my parents and my in-laws whom I hadn't seen them for 10 years. Todd was gracious and worked out the vacation time with me. I was very happy with the way he showed how important it was for me to go on that vacation.

What I am about to share with you is an experience that I will not forget for the rest of my life. Not only that Todd knew the name of my wife, he also knew every member of my family – all the six children – their ages included. Just the night before we had to travel, Todd showed up at my house.

I was excited to welcome him because I knew he was a leader who cared. As we gathered in our living room, he pulled out a nice bag that had some gifts for every member of the family. He expressed appreciation for the type of employee I was and how excited he was that we were going back to Haiti to see our parents. After that he added, "I know you will be traveling with young children. I bring these gifts, so each one can have something to play with in the airplane and while you are traveling. I also bring a gift for you and your wife."

To this day, I can remember how his compassionate act made me feel. My wife and the children were also positively influenced by the goodness of his heart. They could tell that I worked for someone who cared about me and my family.

Needless to say, that when Todd asked his employees to give 100% of their effort, they would respond with 150%.

Todd and I are no longer with Novell, but our relationship continues. Todd knew and demonstrated that in the workplace and in life that people matter first and work second. I know many other leaders and managers who exemplify this principle. I am sure you too know many people in your circle of influence who live this principle. May I invite you to let them know; one more time, how you appreciate their example. May you also be this type of leader at home, in your community, your church, and your work.

Your Thoughts

____

____

____

BUSINESS
Manage tasks and results and lead people.

You are in business because there are people who need your service. If you stop serving them they will find someone else who will.

The things that we do and create can never be greater than the people who create them.
A product can never be greater than its creator.

Your Thoughts

____

____

____

____

BUSINESS

It is noble to work. You don't need to wait for someone to give you work to do. You can create it by serving others.

Your Thoughts

____

____

____

____

Worth of Soul

We are all invincible. There is no reason
to try to destroy another soul.

We are all made of the same material.
It is called soul.

You may not need me, but I need you because
I know how valuable you are to this world.

Your Thoughts

____

____

____

____

♥

JUSTICE AND MERCY

> No mortal being is capable of extending
> the full measure of justice and mercy
> that we all deserve. For that reason,
> it is only fair that we cut one another
> some slack when we judge and be more
> generous when we extend mercy.

Your Thoughts

KNOW THYSELF

> Be your best self. That is all you can be.
> Be true to yourself; for no one else
> knows you that well.

In all circumstances, let your heart be at peace
and your mind calm. Control your emotions,
so you can express your thoughts freely.

We are all born with more talents than we
probably realize. We would do more good
to humanity by cultivating these talents than
dreaming of the ones we wish we had.

Your Thoughts

KNOW THYSELF

Every human being has something to cultivate;
find yours and work on it daily.

The mind can conceive whatever the heart
can feel.

Learn how to be content to live with yourself.
For, this is a companionship that you can't
escape from.

Your Thoughts

____

____

____

____

____

____

SUCCESS AND FAILURE

> Success and failure are twin brothers.
> They frequently walk together. The irony
> is that we can't always tell them apart.

Your Thoughts

COMMUNITY

> Don't forget where you come from. The journey that led you to where you are today began there.

I shared in the beginning of the book a little bit about my background. I grew up in a very small village in Haiti, Departement de L'Artibonite — Arrondissement de Dessalines. The small village is called Sanoix, Commune of Dessalines. I was born from great parents who sacrificed everything for their children. The land in that area is very good to grow rice. Haiti is also known for the excellent rice that is from L'Artibonite — "diri latibonit" as we say it in Creole.

As a child, so many years ago, growing up there, the resources were very limited. They are still limited. I still remember the big trucks (only 3 of them) that transported merchandises and people to the cities. There was no clinic. There was only a very small school for beginners. Life was simple. We made our own toys to play with. We played soccer on every corner we could find. The ball did not have to be round or soft. We did not have soccer cleats. We just played and found ways to entertain ourselves.

We did a lot of chores as well. I loved working on the farm with my father and my brothers. Another chore we had was to watch over the rice that was being dried under the sun. The animals loved to go to get free dinner. Our job was to chase them before they could get to the rice — not always fun. These pigs and goats were smart and fast, but we had to be ready to act before they could strike. I never complained about this task because I kept my eyes focused on the bigger picture. I knew my parents were sacrificing everything to give us a better future. I was ready to do any little thing I could do to contribute and make their lives easier.

At a very young age, I wanted to be a farmer like my father. He was strong and knew how to work the land. He provided for the family. We had food, a roof over our head, and clothes on our backs. With the help of my parents, we were able to attend schools in the city. We started in St. Marc and later moved to Port-au-Prince.

Last December, I checked on YouTube to find the place where I was raised. I felt a sense of gratitude as I contemplated my journey from there and to where I am today. I also felt a greater sense of responsibility.

It became clear to my mind that the place where one is born does not automatically define their human potential or capacity. The choices that we make daily can define the direction we take. We have control over these choices. Wherever we are in life, there is always a light that can guide us to a better way. We need to look to that light and follow it.

I have had great parents who served as a light in my life. I had wonderful and kind neighbors, teachers, and friends who were great examples of that light as well.

I am grateful for where I came from because the journey that led me to where I am today began there. I am grateful for where I am today for it starts the road that will lead me to where I am going to be tomorrow.

Regardles of where you are today, you can lead your life to a higher position by following these simple and practical principles which are a clear vision, a well-defined plan and a willingness to take action as shown in figure 2.

Vision

Have a clear vision of where you want to be. There are many people that serve as examples for you. Seek them out. Keep your eyes and heart fixed on that vision.

Lead your life with a clear vision. I remember vividly that, as a young boy, I wanted to be an engineer — to be specific, an electronic engineer. On my way to school (high school in Haiti) I walked daily by the Faculty of Science, the College of Engineering at the State University of Haiti. Every day I saw the engineering building, I told myself, "one day I will be a student here."

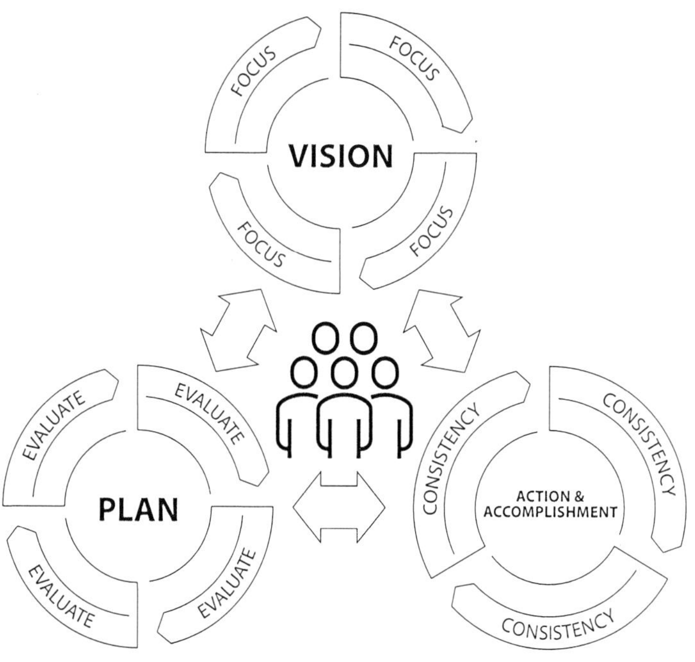

Figure 2

Key Elements for Success in Life

Focus

The vision was clear and I remained focused on it daily. Every decision I made was guided by the big picture. I did not allow myself to get distracted.

Plan

Develop a plan of what it is going to take to accomplish this vision. Make the plan very detailed and specific. Outline the steps you can take today. Identify the people who can help you with the plan. Seek their advice and follow their example. Write the plan and the goal down. Put it somewhere where you can see it daily. Evaluate the plan frequently to make sure it is still aligned with your vision.

Having a clear vision without a well-defined plan is like owning a car that has a strong new engine with a broken transmission or no transmission at all. You might be able to start the car, but you can't go anywhere with it. A lot of people have big dreams, but few people take the time to develop a detailed plan to help them achieve their goal. Your plan needs to be in harmony with your vision. Think again of the car analogy. If the engine of the car is built for a 4-cylinder engine, you don't want to put a transmission that was designed for a 6-cylinder engine.

Evaluate Your Plan

Evaluate your plan regularly to assure that you are doing the tasks that are congruent with your vision. There are times you may need to re-adjust the plan. Think of this scenario: You decided as a family that you are going on a vacation. You identify the location and make the reservation. As a family, you drafted a nice plan. As part of the plan, you agree to drive to your destination. You checked the weather and programmed your GPS to help with the directions. When you are half way you notice that an accident has just taken place and traffic is being rerouted. You still can get to your destination, but it may take more time. In this situation, you have no choice. You must alter your plan a little bit. Things outside of your control can happen.

Action and Accomplishment

Take the necessary action to accomplish your goal. Don't let the resources you don't have keep you from doing the things you can do. Be consistent even in doing little things you can do. Think of it this way. Masons build huge edifice by laying small bricks one at a time.

To progress in life, one must act. I love to watch children learn how to walk. They take incremental steps. They first learn how to stand up. They often use something to help them with their balance. Once they gain a little confidence that they can stand on their own, they are ready to tackle the next step. They do it slowly. As parents and grandparents, we rejoice when we see them trying. We clap. We smile. We encourage them along the process.

Now let us go back to the example of the car. You have a beautiful car, new engine, and a matching transmission. But, you forget to put gas in the engine. You may be smiling at this point. The car won't start. Or if you were on the road and ran out of gas, the car will stop as soon as the gas tank is empty. You have to take the action that will most likely lead you toward your vision. These actions need to be in harmony with your defined plan. If you put water in the gas tank, the car will not start. Putting water in the tank is an activity, but it is the wrong activity. A child that continues to crawl is still doing a lot of activities, but until the child is willing to try standing up and taking steps toward walking, the child will never walk.

Consistency

The best example I can find to illustrate this point is laying bricks. Huge and tall edifices are built with the process of laying one brick at a time. Another example is walking; it doesn't matter if it is a long distance or a short distance — just walk. We take one step at a time. At the end of the day if we were to use a device to measure the steps, we would be impressed at how many steps we took that day. Consistency is the key to our success.

People

There is a reason why the image of people is placed at the center of the graph. People are the central element of everything we do. The first person is you. You need to be able to answer the WHY question for yourself. This applies to the vision, the plan, and the action and accomplishment. You also need to know deep in your heart the positive impact your vision, plan, and action/accomplishment will have on others. You need the people around you to help you achieve your vision. They want you to succeed. You also need to remember that you have a responsibility to add value to their lives.

There are more resources at your disposal that you may not realize. I used to walk one hour each way to go to school when I was in high school in Haiti. My parents could not afford to pay for transportation. I was grateful that they could pay for school, uniform, books, and food, and a place to live. I was grateful that I could go to school when many other children could not. I was grateful that I had two strong legs. I looked forward to going to school with great excitement. Every step on my way to school was a step toward a better life. I did not let the things I did not have keep me from maximizing the blessings I already received. I was happy in my circumstances. That didn't mean I didn't want to change some of them. But, I knew my attitude and action would have an impact on the outcome.

I am a firm believer of doing what you can with what you have. There is a law of attraction and positive energy. There is always something that someone can do. Find out what you can do and do it. No matter how small that simple act is, it is your part to play. It is your contribution to this world. I want to leave this process for you to use as a reminder. It is an effective process that can help you progress from where you are today to where you want to be tomorrow. But you need to start now.

Your Thoughts

____

____

____

____

COMMUNITY

Friends may come and go. But they come in our lives at a specific time and for a specific purpose. For that reason, we need to cherish them and do our best to be a genuine friend.

Your Thoughts

____

____

____

____

COMMUNITY

We decided to come to this earth to exercise our agency. It is wise to learn to be a little bit more patient and tolerant with ourselves and others.

Take time to know people around you.
We all have stories to share and songs to sing.

We all wear a little makeup when we go out into this world. Don't be too quick to judge another person who wears a different shade or color of makeup than you do.

Be patient with the people you know too well. For they may not be that different than the ones you don't know that well and admire.

Your Thoughts

____

____

____

COMMUNITY

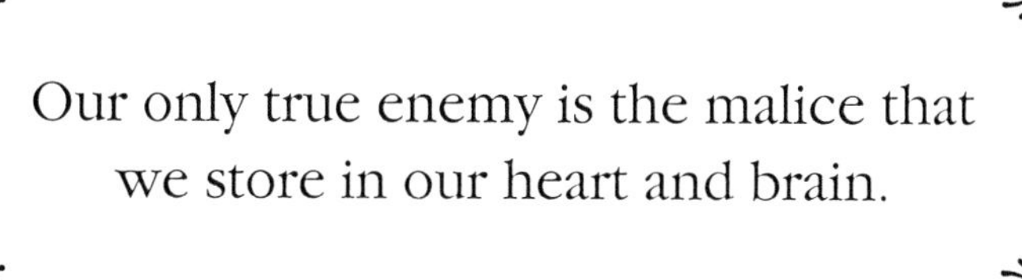

My father had lost his dad when he was a teenager. My grandfather, Manasse was a very well-known person in his community. He was an elegant and well-mannered individual. People described him as being very intelligent and handsome. He was also talented and respected among his peers for having mastered the martial art skills of his era. He loved others and they loved him too. Unfortunately, he did not live long enough to see his posterity. He died before any of his children, (even his oldest son, Estinfort Dort), had any children. My grandpa died at a very young age.

While he did not have any enemies himself, there was a handful of people who were jealous of his success and gifts. He was poisoned. My father loves his dad. As a demonstration of this love, he worked very hard as a young boy to help raise his siblings. Many of his brothers and sisters grew up viewing my dad as their father figure. The oldest brother took on his shoulders the responsibilities of a dad.

My father sacrificed the opportunity of going to school, so he could work on the farm to help raise his siblings. When asked why he made such a great sacrifice he simply responded, "I did it because I love my father. If he was here on earth, he would have provided for all of his children. Since he is not here, I feel the duty to do it."

My father knew very well the circumstances that led to the death of his dad. He even knew the person who killed his father. I grew up missing having my grandpa. I heard so many great things about him. I wish I could have had him around. One day, I asked my father to explain to me the circumstances that led to the death of my grandfather. He shared briefly what happened — where and how it happened. After listening carefully, I pressed him to tell me who did it. I told him it would be nice for us to know, so we could protect ourselves. But, he refused. When he realized I was not too satisfied, he went on to say:

> "Son, I know you miss your grandpa. I can understand why, but I will not tell you who killed him." He continued "I can deal with it, but I am not sure that you can deal with it as a grandchild. There are times you will miss your grandpa so much that you may develop a feeling of revenge. I don't want you to have that feeling. If I plant this feeling in your heart, I will not be able to help you control it."

At that time, I realized how much my father loved his father and how much he loved his children. Since that moment I never had a desire to know who killed my grandpa. My father had taught me a valuable lesson. It is an inter-generational, inter-cultural, and priceless lesson. The lesson I learned is that malice and hate can be the greatest poison one can carry in his heart.

I thank you, my father, for teaching me by your example, one of the greatest lessons in life — to love your enemy and to protect your children against this venomous poison called "hate".

I love you grandpa for having such a wonderful son. May you rest in peace until we meet again in the next life.

COMMUNITY

We are the products of our environment. We also create our own environment. It is wise that we invest a little bit more time in taking care of our environment.

Poverty is a merchandise that society creates. This is the reason it is all around us.

We are all unique. And we are all the same. Isn't that marvelous!

Your Thoughts

____

____

____

____

____

COMMUNITY

Most of us were born with two hands.
Our environment teaches us how to use one
and leaves the other for us to develop.

***

It is not good for man to be selfish. For there is
always plenty to enjoy and some to spare.

Your Thoughts

____

____

____

____

FINANCIAL FREEDOM

The money you have is the money
you save.

Liberate yourself from all types of bondage,
especially financial debts.

Rainy days come in many ways. Prepare for
them so you can have the strength and the
peace to face them.

Your Thoughts

GENERAL

> The human body is the most complex machine that has ever been created. Take good care of it daily, so it can provide a comfortable shelter for your mind and spirit.

I have a wonderful friend who is a mechanic. He has been working on my cars for about 15 years. He is very reliable, dependable, and extremely honest. If he can't solve the problem, he will tell you. He goes the distance to please his clients. He has a great passion and love for cars. He treats them with care.

Let me call him Joe. Joe talks to his clients about the importance of changing the oil, using the highest grade of gasoline, checking the fluid level, making sure the air pressure in the tire is accurate etc. He knows how important these small maintenance checkups are to help the car to run smooth and last longer.

One day we were together at a gas station, he observed a driver who was putting the lowest grade of gasoline in his car. Joe kindly and firmly instructed the man about the damage that the low grade of gas can do to the engine. I could feel his passion for taking care of cars as I watched the look on his face as a result of that person's decision to not pay attention to his advice.

On a different day, Joe was working on my car and was not feeling too well. He told me that he does not like to go to see doctors and is very negligent about his health. He didn't sleep well, or exercise etc. At age 55 he feels like his body is falling apart.

I listened attentively. I like my friend. I would love to see him live a long and healthy life. He is doing so much good for people around him. If cars could talk, they would praise his name for the way he cares for them.

After a moment of reflection, I quickly realized that my friend, Joe, is not alone. It is easy for me to accept that I am too busy to eat lunch or breakfast. I don't exercise the way I should. I am in a good shape and enjoy a relatively good health. But, I am not taking care of my body the way I should. I am trying to be better.

After this eye-opening moment with my friend, I took more time to ponder. How many people do we know know that live such a busy life that they forget to take time to care for their own body? We are not talking about people who have genetic problems. As you probably know, if you run a car without oil for a long time, you will break the engine. It does not matter if the car is new or old.

Where are you today? If you need your legs to be strong enough to hold you as you are getting older, check to see if you are strengthening them today and getting them ready for tomorrow. Are you getting the proper amount of rest? Are you putting the highest grade of nutrients in your body? Are you more concerned about the things of the world that can perish and neglecting the things that matter most?

Wherever we are today, we can do a little better. We can take small steps. We can define some specific goals and a clear vision. We can start performing small consistent actions daily. Recently, I was advised to get rid of 10 unwanted pounds. I made a simple goal to exercise 6 days a week. My exercise routine includes: 15 pushups and 20 sit-ups every morning; drinking water instead of soda; parking my car a little farther away, so I can walk a little more. As you can see, this is not an aggressive goal, but it is working for me. I do these things every day. I can't say that I don't have 5 minutes a day (very maximum) to do 15 pushups and 20 sit-ups.

My routine also includes waking up (I am smiling as I am writing this). Any time I wake up in the morning, it is already a great day. Heavenly Father has already helped me with the first step. I am breathing; life is good; the rest is up to me. After that, I do my daily devotion, fix my bed and exercise before I get in the shower.

After doing these simple things consistently, they become second nature to me. I look forward to doing them. There are many days when I do more than that. But, the key for me is to be consistent. My goal is to keep doing them until the very last day of my life – just like I need air and nutrition until the very last day of my life.

Fifteen and twenty are my numbers. Yours can be 1 or 2. It can also be 30 or 50. It does not matter where you are at this time. You can start there and do your number consistently. You will know when you need to increase the number and the repetition.

Remember that your body is an important gift that you need to treasure every day, every hour and every minute and second.

Your Thoughts

____

____

____

____

GENERAL

We are all servants. We are all masters. Let us treat one another with a little bit more dignity.

Don't believe everything you can see.
Optical illusion is real.

If you don't like where you are going,
you can change course.

Your Thoughts

____

____

____

____

____

____

____

GENERAL

Don't let the things we can quantify keep us
from cherishing the things that we can't.

Not believing in something that exists doesn't
change the fact that it does exist.

A close-minded person is more blind than
someone who is born blind.
For the first can't see and doesn't know it.

Your Thoughts

____

____

____

____

____

____

____

GENERAL
A close-hearted person is colder than ice,

Beware of things that can be sweet like honey
and sting like a bee.

Your Thoughts

Establish and Cultivate Lasting Relationships

I learned many important lessons from my father at an early age. My father was a farmer. He worked hard to be the best farmer he could be and to provide for his family. As a child, I watched him waking up very early in the morning to go to work. I also observed him working long hours. Because of his generosity towards people of his community, he was well-known and respected.

I wanted to be a farmer like him. Being a wise man, he counseled me to focus on getting an education. The first lesson I learned was the importance of helping people you lead focus on having a higher vision and leading them to the path of making that vision a reality. Another lesson I learned from my dad happened when I was working with him in a farm close to our house.

We had taken a short break to enjoy some delicious mangos we just picked from our trees. After I was done eating the mangos I threw the seeds on the ground. My dad, with his gentle voice, said "Son, it would serve you well if you dug a hole in the ground and planted the seed. This seed will grow and one day provide fruits for you and even your family."

At that time, I was not thinking about planting seeds. After all, we had plenty of fruit trees; more fruits than we could consume. Fruit trees were all around me. I thought as a child they will always be there. The thought of planning for tomorrow did not enter my mind until after my father suggested to me to plant the seed.

In life, as in business, it can be easy to focus on today's pressing needs and lose sight of the need to prepare for tomorrow. Even worse we can take for granted things that are readily available to us. We have deadlines to meet, new customers to acquire, and quotas to meet every month or every quarter. Finding time to establish and cultivate relationships that last can be a daunting task. But, any wise mentor or leader would encourage us to take time to work on nurturing our relationships with others. Why is it important that we take time to work on our relationships with others? There are several reasons. One is that we need one another to succeed in this life. Everything we do, we do because we care about the human race.

Recently, I started working on a concept I call Relationship Tree. This idea stems from the principle that all of our accomplishements can be traced back to relationships. I start with any success — small or big. I then, try to trace it back to it's root. It is an exciting exercise. Often the root is very deep and the seed was planted a long time ago. As I work on the relationship tree for each success, I develop a greater appreciation for the people who contributed to that success. You may be a pro in establishing and cultivating relationships that last or you may ask, "how do I start and what do I do?"

Before addressing these questions, let me share some ideas about three important areas. How we treat our relationships with others is crucial. Let me use a fishing analogy. Do you view your relationships as a) catch and release? b) hook and cook? c) catch and cultivate?

a) With the mindset of "catch and release," we tend to size up the person. Some refer to this attitude as relationship arrogance. We make a precipitated judgment before we allow ourselves to know the person. This fish doesn't meet the size I am looking for; therefore, I release it very quickly, so I can focus my energy on bigger fish. Keith Ferrazzi warns us of the danger of spending time or working on relationship with our superior (bosses, people who have what we want) while neglecting to nurture our relationships with people who work for us. If you take time to build a relationship tree, you may find some of the roots of these successes stem from people who are part of a lower step of the ladder. You probably can remember times when you attended an event. You met few people for the first time. You exchanged business cards after a casual conversation. You went home and filed the cards away and never remembered to look at them again.

b) The second one is "hook and cook." People who view relationships in this light are concerned with today's success only. They see it as a transactional relationship. They need to make a one-time sale, so they can meet their quotas. They seldom worry about the person they are working with. It is all about the deal. Life is about themselves and their goals. Don't get me wrong. These people can and do achieve great success in their career. But the road to that success can be lonely and not too enjoyable. They move from transaction to transaction. They never take time to plant seeds in fertile ground.

c) The third level of relationship is what I call "catch and cultivate" or "establish and nurture." Relationships are meant to be nourished and treated with care. When we value something, we treat it with care. We protect it and make sure it can last a long time. A trusted and nurtured relationship is one that can last forever. But, it requires work and constant nourishment.

Like the example of the seed, we need to plant our relationships in good soil. We need to take time to nurture them and even protect them from the elements. How do we do that? And where do we start? Let me address the second question first. You can start within your home and your family. You already have a relationship with these people. You need to take time to nurture that relationship.

It can be easy to take this type of relationship for granted because these are people who are close to you. You may say I already have this in the bag. Next, you can expand to your neighbors and people you associate with at church or in the community. Another group is your co-workers. These are people with whom you spend one-third of your life. After taking time to work on these groups and to practice cultivating relationships that last, you may want to add a few new people per month to your circle of influence. Your customers and other people you do business with could be a great pool.

Now the first question – how do I cultivate and strengthen a relationship? This is a busy life. We are here on earth to be engaged in worthy causes, make valuable contributions to society, and provide for ourselves and loved ones. It is good to be busy. Even in our busy lives, we need to take time to work on the things that matter more.

Before I provide few tips, let me share an experience where I could have done a better job managing my time so I could focus on relationships that matter to me.

Years ago, I was a student in the engineering program at Brigham Young University (BYU). Life was very busy. I had to manage three important tasks: family, school, and work.

A colleague of mine introduced me to his dad who needed assistance with an important and urgent task. I spent hours researching and preparing a document for that person. He appreciated my service and contribution to his cause.

A few years down the road, my wife and I needed to go to Austin, Texas for an important appointment. I called the father of my friend and told him that we are going to Austin, Texas. I asked if he had any contact in that city. He was so happy for the opportunity to serve me. He gave me a name and phone number of one of his close friends who lived in a suburb of Austin.

The friend came to meet us. He and his wife invited us to stay in their home for that night. They took us to our appointment and after that drove us back to the bus station. As a student, our budget was very tight. The generosity of that family meant a lot to us. After we returned home I sent them a thank-you card. The sad part is that I didn't take the time to nurture the relationship with that family and the father of my colleague.

Over time the relationship completely faded out and eventually died. What could I have done to preserve that relationship? I was under the pretext that life was busy. At time, I even thought that these people were too busy. I didn't want to bother them. Looking back, I can see these were only excuses. Without knowing or intending to, I treated these relationships as "catch and release" or even worse as "hook and cook."

As life took me to a higher sphere, I began to understand better the importance of relationship. I should have learned this principle from my father, but I didn't. But it isn't too late. Over the years, I have managed to do a better job. I still have a ways to go, but I am working on it daily.

Here are a few tips that can help you establish, manage, and cultivate relationships that last.

- Remember and respect names - When you meet someone, make a concerted effort to know and remember their name. Treat the name with reverence for this is the most important word in their vocabulary. If the name is difficult and unique, I find a way to pay that person a genuine compliment about having a unique name. If the name is common like John, I tell myself that that person I am conversing with is a unique John. While there are several people whose name is John, there is one "This John." I show respect to the name and the person.

- Learn pertinent information - try to learn and remember something about that person. Next time you interact with that person you want to find something to make that conversation more personable.

- Take notes - when it is appropriate, jot down some information about that person; like children names, hobbies, or even birthdays — whatever they are willing to share.

- Look for an opportunity to serve - do something just because. Serve without expecting anything in return.

- Be humble - allow others to help you if you need assistance — it is OK to ask for help.

- Perform simple acts of kindness — send a simple text or an email on special occasions such as Christmas, Valentine's Day, Father's Day, Mother's Day or on their birthday.

- Use technology and social media - LinkedIn offers an awesome vehicle for managing and cultivating relationships.

- Do some "just because" acts - send an email, text or a hand-written card just because you are thinking of that person.

- Express a kind word of encouragement or appreciation - this one does not cost anything, but it's priceless. It can brighten our day. It can lift the heart and the soul. It can inspire the human spirit. There are plenty of opportunities to express your gratitude. The more we give it away, the more of it we have to give.

- Add yours ____

____

____

____

A relationship is like a fruit seed. We need to plant it in fertile soil. We need to take time to nourish it constantly. We need to protect it from the elements. We need to be patient. As we do so, we can be sure that it will bear delicious fruit. In daily life and in business, let us do our best to cultivate relationships that have the power to transform the lives of the people around us and lift their spirit to a higher sphere.

Let us remember this wisdom. We are made up of all the people who have touched and influenced our lives for good. Everyone who has lifted our hearts during moments of discouragement, spoken kind words to us when life is difficult, or encouraged us to keep on trying, became a part of who we are today. Today is the time to start working on improving our relationships with others. Our family is the place to begin. A kind word of encouragement and a good deed is a currency we all can afford.

A Moment of Reflection

I have always loved the month of July. As a child growing up in Haiti, I looked forward to summer vacation with great anticipation and excitement. July was my favorite time in the summer. It was the time to work in the field with my father and my brothers. Having lived in the United States for over 30 years I have found other reasons to love July. It is the time that Americans reserve to celebrate the independence of a great nation.

During the week of the 4th of July, my thoughts are with the men and women who have sacrificed all, even their own lives, so that all who live in this great land can enjoy the fruits of liberty. Many have also sacrificed their lives, so people in other nations can have the blessing of living in a free land. I have been reflecting on the sacrifices of those who are currently serving in the military whether they are stationed overseas or serving in their own cities or states. They serve with valor and courage. They serve to protect the weakest and the strongest among us. They do it for the benefits of those who recognize and appreciate their efforts as well as for those who don't show any gratitude for their service.

Another reason I love the month of July is that it offers me the opportunity to reflect on the sacrifices that pioneers have made. Wherever we live, we benefit from the sacrifices of those who paved the way for us. I have heard once that we breathe the air that we didn't create and cross bridges that we didn't build. My wife and I visited Saint Pete Beach, Florida, last year. Every day we entered the town and crossed a beautiful long bridge that connects the Tampa Bay area to the southern part of Florida. I was amazed at the labor and the engineering required to build that bridge. It would not be too extreme to think that there are many who take crossing that bridge daily for granted.

I always marvel at the sacrifices that the Mormon pioneers made to cross the plains during difficult times and seasons and under the most dangerous circumstances. (In your own culture, you also know pioneers that exemplified this spirit of sacrifice.) Many perished before they could reach their final destination. The pioneers who were able to make it didn't find a land of honey and mana. They had to till the soil, pave the roads, and build bridges. They found a desolate place close to a salty lake. They worked hard. They had a vision. They had faith in the Almighty God. While I don't have any relatives who were part of this group, I cherish daily their bravery. As a resident of Utah, I am grateful for their sacrifices.

Another groups of pioneers that we often neglect to recognize are those who are currently laying the foundation for future generations as well as those who devote their time and resources in humanitarian services. Many of them live quietly among us. They often left their comfort zones to serve those who live in deplorable conditions. For the last 16 years I have had the distinct privilege of working with fellow humanitarians who go to Haiti and Dominican Republic to offer health service to children and adults who so desperately need this service. These volunteers donate their time, talents, and also pay for their own expenses. They also help cover the cost to buy medications and supplies.

Other generous people who can't go on these humanitarian services offer their financial support, so we can purchase needed medications, supplies and equipment. I watch how these volunteers and donors work together in the spirit of love and humanity to alleviate the pain and the suffering of others and to give them hope. They come from all walks of life and religious backgrounds. They give their all and ask for nothing in return. They too serve as my heroes and people I look up to every day.

As we take time to reflect on how blessed we are to live in this beautiful land of liberty, let us also take time to remember daily those who sacrificed all, so we can enjoy these blessings. Let us continue to lift the lives of the people around us. For this life is given to us as a gift that we must share with others.

With much respect and gratitude for all past, present, and future pioneers and military men and women who make this world a better place for all.

One Final Note

I trust you have enjoyed these thoughts and the events that inspired them. You are a special soul with a special mission. Find your passion and do it with compassion. Take a moment each day, before you retire, to appreciate the blessings you received and the lessons learned that day. Remember your thoughts help shape your action.

May you think and act daily with a compassionate heart and lift the lives of the people around you. I wish you great success in your endeavors.

REFLECT > RECORD > REMEMBER > APPLY > SHARE

Your friend!

Illens

121

Sources

John C. Maxwell – Online Courses

About the Author

Illens Dort grew up on a farm in a small town in Haiti. He grew up in very humble circumstances, but he was fortunate to have parents who sacrificed everything to help him receive a formal education. Even as a child, Illens longed to help children in deplorable situations. He saw many children who woke up every day without knowing when or where their next meal would come from. As a student at the University of Haiti, he accepted a part time job to teach math at the College Isidor Jean-Louis in Port-au-Prince. It was at that time that he had an experience with a student that changed his life forever.

One day, during his class, he noticed a student who was unusually quiet. Something had to be wrong with him. Illens approached the young man and asked, "Jean, I noticed that you did not participate at all in class and you were extremely quiet. Is everything ok?" The young man responded;

"I have not had anything to eat for 3 days." Illens' heart sank. Fortunately, he had one Haitian dollar that he intended to use for transportation home. Illens reached into his pocket, pulled out the money and gave it to the young man saying, "Take this to your mother so she can buy food for you and your siblings."

The look on the student's face displayed an expression of deliverance and gratitude. Illens walked home that day grateful to know that there would be food on his own table and absorbed by the fact that there were thousands of other children like that young man who lived in the same circumstances throughout Haiti and the Dominican Republic. Then he began to understand what his father used to say: "Son, one of the most satisfying meals you will ever eat in your lifetime is one that you will share with someone in need."

From Haiti to Utah

After serving an LDS mission in Haiti, Illens came to the United States. He attended Snow College and then transferred to BYU where he earned a bachelor of science in Electronic Engineering Technology and later received an MBA at the University of Phoenix. Illens is also a graduate of Goldman Sachs 10,000 Small Businesses.

Speaker - Trainer - Coach

Illens Dort is a speaker, trainer, coach, and mentor with a passion for helping people find their passion and do it with compassion. He is also a member of The John Maxwell Team; an elite group of speakers, coaches, trainers, and mentors. He speaks on a number of topics: Building and Investing in Human Capital, Establish and Cultivate Lasting Relationships, Authentic and Transformational Leadership, Leading with Passion and Compassion, The 7 Universal Laws of Community.

Entrepreneur

He is the founder of Lift a Life, a nonprofit organization that focuses on healthcare and vocational training to help children and families who live in underserved communities in Dominican Republic and

Haiti. The organization has helped over 36,000 people. Lift a Life has a full-service clinic and a vocational school in Bayaguana, Dominican Republic. He is the CEO and founder of HumanEkdromi, a company that focuses on humanitarian excursions, corporate training, and executive retreats.

Contact

For More information about Illens Dort and to hire him for coaching or speaking visit www.IllensDort.com. Illens Dort is a passionate and dynamic speaker who keeps his audience engaged whether it is a small group of 30 or a large group of over 1000. If you are looking for a speaker who can connect with your nonprofit fundraising events, or you need someone to inspire your team, Illens is your man. Illens can tailor his message to fit your specific needs and the composition of your audience.

LinkedIn and Facebook.

facebook.com/illens.dort

linkedin.com/in/illens-dort-4790291

Endorsements

Illens Dort brings us original and authentic aphorisms that are powerful technologies to enable us to gain access to our higher self. They not only help us to gain access to our intelligence of the mind and heart, they also help us gain access to the intelligence of the will. So by understanding these aphorisms we may achieve what is in our will. May the will be done!

— Leila Akwabi & Macharia Waruingi
  Ustawi Biomedical Research Innovation and Industrial
  Centers of Africa [UBRICA]

It is our life experiences that make us who we are and give our life meaning. Illens' life work focuses on helping each of us realize our potential and begin to believe again. It is his mission in life to help business owners become visionaries, employees become partners, and the less-fortunate become producers. In this book, Illens shares thoughts that have inspired his journey in life. I invite you to walk with him as he attempts to do his part to make the world a better place."

— Mark Ishii -
  Founder and CEO - Ishii Design